Samantha's Friendship Fun

American Girl

Table of Contents

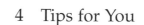

If you've read the stories about Samantha, you know that life for girls growing up in the early 1900s was different than it is for girls today. But some things about growing up haven't changed at all. Girls still love to spend time with their friends playing games, making crafts and artwork, and cooking treats. In fact, having fun with friends is still one of the best parts about being a girl, just as it was for Samantha and Nellie.

Learning about the crafts, meals, and games of Samantha's time will help you understand what it was like to grow up the way she did. Enjoying these activities of the past with your friends will bring history to life for you and your friends today.

Tips for You

General Tips

 *The most important tip is to **work with an adult.** When you see this symbol, it means you will need an adult's help with that step.*

- *Read all the directions before you start.*
- *Wash your hands with soap before and after your project. Wear an apron, tie back your hair, and roll up your sleeves.*
- *Don't use the stove or oven without an adult's supervision. Turn off the stove burners or oven as soon as you are done.*
- *Be careful with sharp knives and scissors.*
- *Put covers back on containers tightly. If you spill, clean up right away.*
- *Leave your work area as clean as you found it. Wash dishes, put away supplies, and throw away garbage.*

Cooking Tips

1. Get an adult's help when the directions tell you to, or if you're not sure what to do. Have an adult help you use cooking equipment properly.

2. Before you start to cook, gather everything you will need. Set the ingredients and utensils where you can reach them easily.

3. When you stir or mix, hold the bowl or pan steady on a flat surface, not in your arms.

4. Use pot holders when touching hot pans, to protect yourself from burns. Protect countertops by using trivets under hot pots and pans.

5. Keep hot foods hot and cold foods cold. If you plan to make things early and serve them later, store them properly. Foods that could spoil belong in the refrigerator. Wrap foods well.

Craft Tips

1  Get an adult's help when the directions tell you to, or if you're not sure what to do. Have an adult help you use tools properly.

2 You can find most of the materials listed in this book in your home or at craft and fabric stores. If an item is starred (*), look at the bottom of the materials list to read more about it or find out where you can get it. Gather all your supplies before you start.

3 Select a good work area for your craft projects. Pick a place that has plenty of light and is out of reach of pets and little brothers and sisters.

4 Ask your friends to bring aprons or smocks. Have everyone tie back her hair and roll up her sleeves. Cover the work area with newspapers.

5 If there's a step that doesn't make sense to you, try it out with a piece of scrap paper or fabric first. Practicing often helps.

6 If the crafts don't turn out exactly like the pictures in the book, that's perfectly all right! The pictures are just there to give you ideas. Crafts become more meaningful when you add your own personal touch.

Sewing Tips

Threading the Needle
Wet one end of the thread in your mouth. Push the thread through the eye of the needle.

Pull about 5 inches of thread through the needle. Then tie a double knot near the end of the long tail of thread.

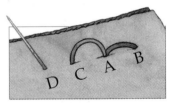

Sewing a Backstitch
Bring the needle up at A. Go down at B. Come up at C and go down at A. Come up at D and go down at C. Keep going!

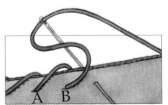

Sewing a Whipstitch
Bring the needle up at A. Pull the thread over the edge of the fabric, and come up at B. Keep going!

Samantha's Life and Times

In Samantha's day, there were lots of rules of *etiquette*, or proper behavior. In 1904, a ten-year-old girl named Virginia Carey Hudson wrote this in her diary: *"Etiquette is what you are doing and saying when people are looking and listening. What you are thinking . . . is your business. Thinking is not etiquette."*

Whole books were written to tell girls what the etiquette was for every situation. A girl like Samantha would never just tumble out of bed and come to breakfast in her pajamas. Each morning, Samantha had to dress in a clean, freshly pressed dress, tie a fluffy hairbow in her neatly brushed hair, and walk, not run, downstairs to breakfast with Grandmary.

During the school year, Samantha attended Miss Crampton's Academy for Young Ladies. She studied subjects like arithmetic, history, and spelling, but she also had lessons on being a proper young lady. For example, she had to practice walking with books balanced on her head so she would learn how to move with perfect posture and grace!

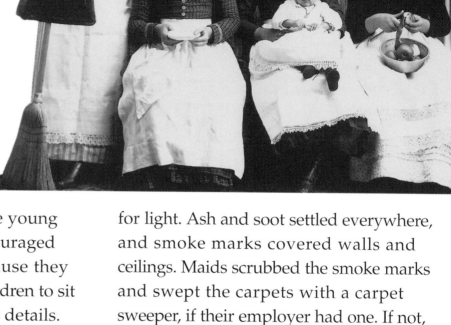

Servants like these washed and ironed the dresses Samantha wore, cooked the meals she ate, and warmed her bed with a hot water bottle if the night was chilly. They made it possible for Samantha to enjoy an elegant and proper life.

In the late afternoon, Samantha spent time with Grandmary in the parlor. Samantha made sure she looked presentable—no floppy hairbow, droopy stockings, or scuffy shoes allowed! When Samantha entered the parlor, she curtsied to Grandmary and quietly sat down to practice her needle-work, an important skill for fine young ladies to learn. People also encouraged girls to take piano lessons because they believed these lessons taught children to sit up straight and pay attention to details.

One of the most *improper* things a well-bred young lady could do was work—even in her own home. A girl like Samantha never had to set a table or dry a dish or make a bed. Servants did all those things, and much more. Cleaning a house in Samantha's time was more work than it is today. People used fireplaces for heat, and gas or oil lamps for light. Ash and soot settled everywhere, and smoke marks covered walls and ceilings. Maids scrubbed the smoke marks and swept the carpets with a carpet sweeper, if their employer had one. If not, they got down on their knees and brushed the carpets by hand.

Where did all these ideas about what was proper come from?

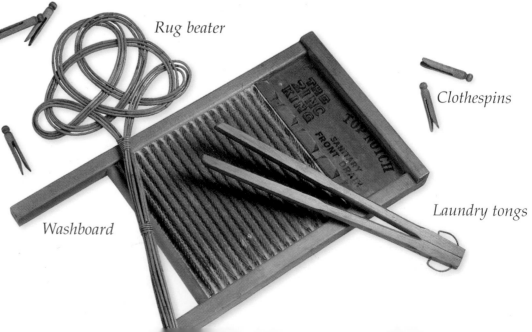

Rug beater

Clothespins

Washboard

Laundry tongs

In the early 1900s, England was a powerful empire, ruling many countries all over the world. Americans admired the success of the English and wanted to be just like them. Wealthy Americans paid close attention to what wealthy English people wore, what they ate, and, most importantly, how they behaved. Upper-class English manners became the model for what was proper in American society. Fashionable Americans dressed elegantly for dinner each evening, served tea in the afternoon, and went *calling*, or visiting friends, just as people did in England.

Tea was always served in the afternoon.

When Samantha was growing up, Americans were fascinated by Queen Victoria, shown here with Prince Albert and their children. She ruled England from 1837 to 1901. Queen Victoria became so popular that the time of her rule is still known as the Victorian Age.

Afternoon Calls

Once a week, Samantha went with Grandmary as she paid social calls to her friends and acquaintances. Samantha wore her best dress and a big fluffy hairbow, and she carried her own elegant calling cards.

Grandmary also received callers each week. When visitors came to call, Mr. Hawkins, the butler, answered the door. He showed the visitors into the front hall, where they waited while he announced them to Grandmary. If Grandmary was accepting callers, Mr. Hawkins showed them into the parlor. Grandmary and Samantha always offered their visitors dainty sandwiches and petits fours to nibble as they chatted.

Samantha had to be on her very best behavior during social calls. If she tried to slip into the parlor late, Grandmary was most displeased!

Pay a Proper Call

Pay a call just as Samantha might have done in 1904. Make elegant calling cards to bring with you, too! In Samantha's time, people set aside "at-home days" to receive callers. Today, you should arrange your visit ahead of time.

1 Dress in your very best—a clean dress, shiny shoes, and a pretty hairbow. Make sure not a hair is out of place.

Step 1

2 Do not sit in the best seat unless your hostess seats you there. Sit up straight and tall. No fidgeting!

Step 2

3 Discuss only subjects of interest to everyone. It is not proper to discuss your health or clothing, politics, money, or diseases. Stay only 15 minutes.

4 A proper way to take your leave is to say, "Miss _____, your company is so agreeable that I am staying longer than I intended. But I hope to have the pleasure of seeing you again soon."

Getting Dressed

How long does it take you to get dressed in the morning? For Samantha, getting dressed was a big job. Imagine how much time it would take to put on all these things:

1. A long, frilly under-shirt called a *chemise*

2. A pair of lace-trimmed *drawers*, or underpants

3. At least one lacy *petticoat*

4. Long cotton or woolen *stockings*

5. *Garters* to hold up your stockings

6. A fancy ruffled *dress*

7. High-button *shoes*

8. A starched white *pinafore*

9. A fluffy *hairbow*

10. In winter, a red flannel *petticoat* and *long underwear*, too!

A girl's dress and grooming showed her family's place in society.

13

The Latest Frills

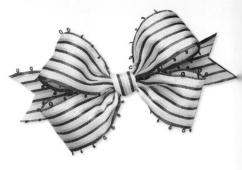

Proper young ladies in Samantha's time always kept their long hair neatly pulled back with huge, jaunty bows!

Materials

For You

- Scissors
- 1¼ yards of stiff ribbon, 2 to 3 inches wide
- A French clip barrette at least 2½ inches long

For Your Doll

- ¾ yard of ribbon, 1 to 2 inches wide
- A French clip barrette at least 1½ inches long

1 Make your hairbow first. Cut the ribbon into 3 equal pieces.

2 Take 2 of the strips. Fold the ends of each strip into the middle to form two "bows."

3 Lay 1 of the bows across the other at an angle, scrunching them in the middle.

14

4 Open the barrette. Center the bows over the top part of the barrette.

5 Tie the third strip around the bows and the top of the barrette. Cut the ends of the ribbon to make a V shape.

6 Fluff out the bows. Now make a second hairbow so you and your doll can dress like proper young ladies!

Calling Cards

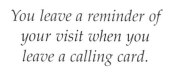

*You leave a reminder of
your visit when you
leave a calling card.*

Materials

- Scissors
- Magazines or
  greeting cards
- Glue
- Stick-on decorations
  (optional)
- Unlined cards,
  3 by 4 inches
- Pencil
- Black felt-tip pen
- Small bowl
- Foam paintbrush,
  1 inch wide

1 Cut out small pictures from old
magazines or greeting cards, or get
pretty stick-on decorations. Glue one
or two onto each card.

2 Use a pencil to write your name lightly
on each card. Trace over your signature
with a black pen. Let the ink dry.

3 Squeeze a little glue into the bowl. Use
the foam paintbrush to brush a thin coat
of glue over each card. When the glue
dries, you are ready to go calling!

CALLING CARD MESSAGES

If a girl or lady paid a call on someone who was not receiving visitors or was away, she would leave her card to show that she had stopped by. A well-bred lady *never* wrote notes on her calling cards—but she could say a lot just by the way she folded her card!

Here are some of the calling-card messages that Samantha and Grandmary would have understood:

- *If the lower right corner of the card was folded, it meant "Good-bye. I'll be away for a while."*

- *If the upper left corner was folded, it meant "Congratulations!"*

- *A folded lower left corner expressed sympathy on the death of a loved one.*

- *If the whole left end of the card was folded, it showed that the caller had come to call on all the ladies and girls in the family, not just the person she knew best.*

*Visitors left their calling cards in a special dish called a **card receiver**.*

Social Calls

Proper girls and ladies in the early 1900s practiced their elegant manners when they paid *social calls*, or visits, to friends and acquaintances. Women kept records of calls paid, received, and owed, just the way people keep track of paying bills.

Calls were always paid to the lady of a house, and they were an important way to show respect to her. If a call was not paid, the person felt *snubbed,* or treated with disrespect. Snubbing someone could be serious business. One woman remembered walking along the street and seeing a house on fire. Her first thought was to warn the owner. Then she remembered that the woman who lived in the burning house had owed her a call for some time, so she decided to continue on her way!

Fancy Fan

Stay cool the same way Samantha did, with a pretty paper fan!

Materials

- Sheet of gift wrap, 30 by 4 inches
- 2 heavy books
- Ruler
- Stapler
- Foam paintbrush, 1 inch wide
- Acrylic paint, any color
- 2 flat sticks, 8 inches by ½ inch
- White glue
- Rubber band
- 6-inch piece of satin ribbon, 1 inch wide

1 Lay the sheet of gift wrap on a table with the back side facing up. Place a heavy book at each end of the gift wrap overnight to flatten it.

2 Remove the books, and then fold one end of the paper over 1 inch.

Step 2

3 Turn over the paper and make another fold 1 inch from your first fold. Keep folding until you reach the end of your paper.

Step 3

4 Staple the fan together, about ¼ inch from one end.

5 Now make a handle for your fan. Paint each flat stick on one side. Let the paint dry, and then paint the other side of each stick. Paint the edges, too.

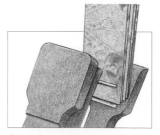

Step 4

6 When the paint is dry, glue 1 flat stick to one of the outside folds of the fan, 1/4 inch above the staple.

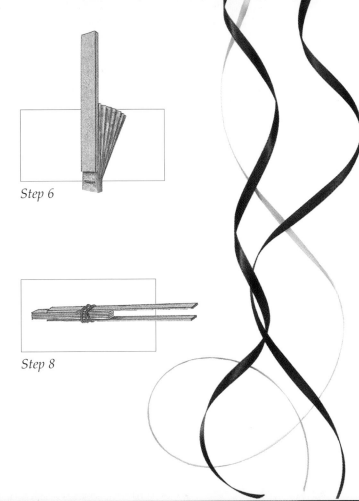

Step 6

7 Glue the other flat stick to the other outside fold in the same way.

8 Wrap a rubber band around the fan to keep it closed until the glue is dry.

Step 8

9 When the glue is dry, open your fan. Tie the ribbon around the handle to keep the fan open, and untie the ribbon when you want it closed.

Keeping Cool

Fans were elegant accessories for young ladies during the hot summer months. They were useful, too. There was no air-conditioning in 1904!

Jelly Biscuits

These teatime treats have a spoonful of jelly baked right in!

Ingredients

- 2 cups flour
- 4 teaspoons baking powder
- 2 tablespoons sugar
- ½ teaspoon salt
- ½ cup shortening
- ¾ cup milk
- Flour for cutting board and rolling pin
- ½ cup jelly or jam

Equipment

- Sifter
- Medium mixing bowl
- Measuring cups and spoons
- Pastry cutter (optional)
- Fork
- Cutting board
- Rolling pin
- 2- to 3-inch round cookie cutter or drinking glass
- Spatula
- Cookie sheet
- 1-inch round cookie cutter or bottle cap
- Pot holders

Serves 6

1 Preheat the oven to 425°.

2 Put the sifter into the mixing bowl. Measure the flour, baking powder, sugar, and salt into the sifter. Then sift them into the bowl.

Step 2

3 Add the shortening. Use the pastry cutter or a fork to blend the shortening and flour mixture until it looks like coarse crumbs.

Step 3

4 Add the milk and stir it in with the fork until the mixture forms a soft ball of dough.

5 Sprinkle a little flour on the cutting board. Spread it evenly with your hands.

6 Put the ball of dough on the cutting board and knead it 12 times. To knead the dough, press down on it firmly with the heels of your hands. Then fold it in half. Press it and fold it again. Add a little more flour if the dough sticks.

Step 6

7 Put more flour on the cutting board and rolling pin. Roll out the dough from the center to the edges until it is about 1/4 inch thick.

Step 7

8 With the large cookie cutter or the glass, cut circles close together out of the dough.

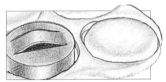
Step 8

9 Use the spatula to move half the circles to the cookie sheet. Place them 1 inch apart.

10 With the small cookie cutter or bottle cap, cut a hole in the center of the remaining circles. Lift these rings onto the top of the circles on the cookie sheet.

Step 10

11 Form a ball with the remaining dough, roll it out, and continue forming circles and rings until all the dough is used.

12 Put a teaspoon of jelly or jam into each ring.

13 Bake the jelly biscuits for 12 to 15 minutes, until they are golden brown. Have an adult remove the biscuits from the oven to cool.

Step 12

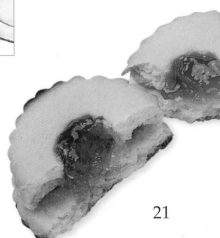

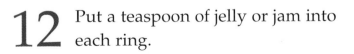

21

Petits Fours

Impress your guests with elegant, bite-size cakes, frosted in pretty pastels.

Ingredients

- A frozen pound cake or sheet cake
- 1 can (1 lb.) white ready-made frosting
- 2 tablespoons milk
- Food coloring
- Decorator frosting in tubes

Equipment

- Sharp knife
- Mixing spoons
- Mixing bowl
- Measuring spoon
- Small bowls, one for each color frosting
- Waxed paper
- Cookie tray or large dinner plate
- Spreading knife

Makes about 32

1 While the cake is still frozen, have an adult help you cut it into small rectangles, about 1 inch by 2 inches.

2 Spoon the white frosting into the mixing bowl. Add the milk and stir until the frosting is smooth and glossy.

3 Divide the frosting into small bowls, one for each color frosting.

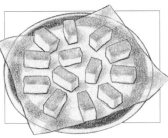
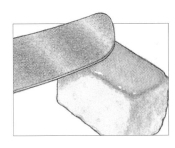

4 Squeeze 1 or 2 drops of food coloring into each bowl. Mix well, using a separate spoon for each color frosting.

5 Place waxed paper on the cookie tray or plate. Arrange your cakes on top. Space the cakes evenly so they do not touch.

6 Spread the colored frosting on your cakes. Try to make the frosting cover each cake smoothly.

7 Place the frosted cakes in the freezer for 30 minutes. Afterward, use tubes of decorator frosting to decorate the cakes with squiggles, swirls, and dots!

Chicken Salad Sandwiches

Chicken salad was a favorite in Samantha's time, just as it is today.

Ingredients

- 2 cups cooked or canned chicken
- 2 celery ribs
- 2 hard-boiled eggs, peeled
- 2 tablespoons pickle relish
- 4 tablespoons mayonnaise
- Salt and pepper
- Softened butter
- 12 slices of bread

Equipment

- Sharp knife
- Cutting board
- Medium mixing bowl
- Measuring cups and spoons
- Wooden spoon
- Butter knife

Serves 6

1. Have an adult help you cut the chicken into very small cubes.

2. Have an adult help you cut off the ends of the celery ribs and chop the ribs into very small pieces. Cut the hard-boiled eggs into small pieces.

3. Put the chicken, celery, and eggs into the bowl. Add pickle relish, mayonnaise, and a sprinkle of salt and pepper. Mix well.

4. Butter 6 slices of bread. Spread the chicken salad on the buttered slices.

5. Put the remaining 6 slices of bread on top. Cut away the crusts. Then cut the sandwiches into triangles, squares, or rectangles.

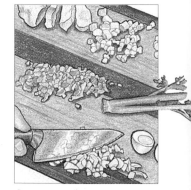

Steps 1 and 2

Cream Cheese and Walnut Sandwiches

These rich, dainty sandwiches are scrumptious for tea.

Ingredients

- 8 ounces cream cheese, softened
- ¼ cup chopped walnuts
- ⅛ teaspoon nutmeg
- 1 tablespoon cream
- 4 tablespoons butter, softened
- 1 teaspoon honey
- 12 slices of bread

Equipment

- 2 small mixing bowls
- Measuring cups and spoons
- Fork
- Mixing spoon
- Cutting board
- Butter knife
- Sharp knife

Serves 6

1 Place the cream cheese in one of the bowls. Add the chopped walnuts, nutmeg, and cream. Stir well with the fork.

2 Place the butter in the other bowl. Add the honey and mix well with the spoon.

3 Lay 6 slices of bread on the cutting board. Use the butter knife to spread the honey-butter on the bread. Then spread the cream cheese and nut filling on top.

4 Lay the remaining 6 slices of bread on top of the filling. Use the sharp knife to cut off the crusts. Then cut each sandwich into triangles, squares, or rectangles.

Lem🍋n Ice

*Zesty lemon ice makes
a perfect refreshment
on a warm day!*

Ingredients

- 4 lemons
- 1 orange
- 4 cups water
- 1½ cups sugar

Equipment

- Sharp knife
- Cutting board
- Juicer
- Bowl to fit juicer
- Measuring cups
- 2-quart saucepan
- Wooden spoon
- Large mixing bowl
- Strainer
- Plastic container
  with lid
- Large metal spoon

Serves 6–8

1 Have an adult help you cut the lemons and orange in half on the cutting board.

2 Set the juicer over the bowl so the edges fit tightly.

3 Squeeze the juice out of the lemon and orange halves by turning them back and forth on the juicer while pushing down.

4 Measure the water and sugar into the saucepan. Stir them well.

5 Heat the mixture over medium heat until it *boils*, or bubbles rapidly, for 10 minutes.

Step 1

Step 3

6 Have an adult help you pour the water and sugar mixture into the large mixing bowl.

7 Pour the juice through the strainer into the mixing bowl. Stir the mixture well. Then let it cool.

8 Pour the mixture into the plastic container and cover it. Put it in the freezer and leave it there for several hours, until the mixture is frozen solid.

9 Use the large spoon to scrape shavings off the top of the lemon ice and shape them into scoop-size servings.

Ice Delivery

*Before people had refrigerators, blocks of ice were delivered to homes in horse-drawn wagons. Deliverymen used large tongs to pick up the ice and lift it onto their shoulders. Then they carried the ice into kitchens like Samantha's and put it into the **icebox.** On hot summer days, the iceman would give children chips of ice as cool treats!*

Sunday Brunch

Every Sunday morning, Mrs. Hawkins made brunch for Samantha and Grandmary. But one Sunday was special— Uncle Gard and Aunt Cornelia were visiting! Samantha wanted the table to look festive, so she made a pretty basket and filled it with fresh flowers from the garden. She put it right in the center of the table. Then Samantha helped Mrs. Hawkins plan the menu, just like a proper hostess should. They were going to have strawberries from the garden, slices of juicy ham, cheesy omelets, and fresh-baked blueberry muffins. Samantha knew it would be delicious!

Flower Basket

Make a beautiful basket to decorate your table!

Materials

- Pencil
- Sheet of tracing paper
- Newspaper
- Piece of white poster board, 12 inches square
- Scissors
- White glue
- 6 paper clips
- Foam paintbrush, 1 inch wide
- Acrylic paints, any colors
- Small artist's paintbrush
- Any of the following: lace, ribbon, gold or silver foil, small cutout pictures

1 Use the pencil to trace the basket and handle patterns shown on page 92 onto tracing paper. Don't cut out the patterns.

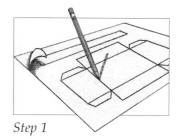
Step 1

2 Place the sheet of tracing paper on the newspaper, design side down. Use the side of the pencil to color over the backs of the patterns.

Step 2

3 Place the tracing paper on the poster board, design side up. Then draw over the lines of the patterns, pressing firmly.

4 Lift the tracing paper. The pencil markings from the back of the tracing paper will come off where you traced.

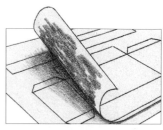
Step 4

5 Cut out the poster-board patterns. Lay the basket pattern on a table, design side up.

6 Fold up the small flaps, and fold up the short sides of the basket. Then fold up the long sides of the basket.

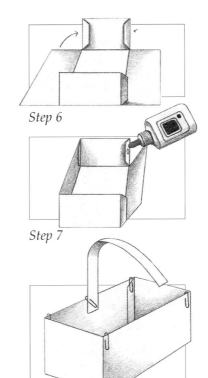

Step 6

Step 7

7 Squeeze 3 small dots of glue onto the outside of each flap. Glue the flaps to the insides of the long sides of the basket.

8 Slip paper clips over the flaps to hold them in place while the glue dries.

9 Glue one end of the handle to one of the long sides of the basket as shown. Slip a paper clip over the handle.

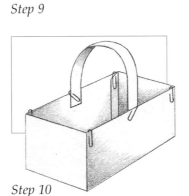

Step 9

10 Bend the handle and glue it to the other long side of the basket. Slip another paper clip over the handle.

11 Let the glue dry for about 15 minutes, and then remove the paper clips.

Step 10

12 Use the foam paintbrush to give your basket a base coat of paint.

13 When the paint is dry, add other painted decorations with the artist's paintbrush, or decorate the basket with lace, ribbon, foil, or cutout pictures.

Stand-Up Napkins

Let elaborately folded cloth napkins greet your guests at the table. One traditional shape, called the **Bishop's Hat,** can be dressed up several ways.

Materials

• Large square cloth napkins (20 inches by 20 inches work best), one for each place setting

1 Lay a napkin flat on the table and fold it in half diagonally to form a triangle. Then turn the napkin so the folded edge is closest to you.

Step 1

2 Fold the right and left corners up so they meet at the top point.

Step 2

3 Fold the newly created bottom point up, until it's about 1 inch below the top point.

Step 3

4 Fold the same point back down to the bottom edge.

Step 4

5 Carefully turn the napkin over, then fold the left corner about 1/3 of the way toward the right corner.

Step 5

6 Fold the right corner over the left corner, and then tuck the point into the fold so the bottom forms a tube that will not pop open.

Step 6

7 Stand the napkin up. With all the points straight up, this is called a Bishop's Hat, a name that refers to the tall, elaborate hats worn by Catholic bishops.

8 You can also create a napkin that looks like a butterfly or bird in flight by gently pulling down the left and right sides in front of the point until they are horizontal.

9 To create another variation that looks like a blooming plant, gently fold down the left and right sides and tuck the points into the fold around the middle of the napkin. Then tuck a flower into the center of the napkin, as shown.

Step 7

Step 8

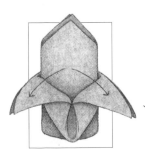
Step 9

No Simple Matter

In Samantha's time, attending a formal dinner was no simple matter. When Samantha sat down at the table, she first had to make sense of all the silverware. There were separate forks for fish, meat, and salad. There was a meat knife and a fish knife. In addition, there was a

A proper table setting

soup spoon, a tiny salt spoon, and often a little fork just for raw oysters.

And what would Samantha eat with all that silverware? At the turn of the century, French cooking was all the rage. Wealthy Americans wanted their cooks to make fashionable French dishes, beginning with soup and ending with nuts. In between, there were courses of fish, roast beef, salad, sometimes duck or pheasant, fruit, and several fancy desserts!

These students are learning how to set a proper table.

33

Blueberry Muffins

Fresh-baked muffins filled with tart, plump blueberries are a traditional breakfast favorite.

Ingredients

- Shortening to grease muffin pan
- 1 cup fresh blueberries
- 3 tablespoons shortening
- 3 tablespoons sugar
- 1 egg
- 1 cup milk
- 1¾ cups flour
- 3 teaspoons baking powder
- ¾ teaspoon salt
- Butter and jam

Equipment

- Muffin pan
- Strainer
- Paper towels
- Measuring cups and spoons
- Large mixing bowl
- Wooden spoon
- Sifter
- Pot holders
- Toothpick
- Basket or plate

Serves 4–6

1 Preheat the oven to 400°. Lightly grease each muffin cup with a bit of shortening.

2 Put the blueberries into the strainer, and then rinse them under cold running water. Drain them on paper towels.

3 Measure 3 tablespoons of shortening into the mixing bowl. Slowly stir the sugar into the shortening until the mixture is light and fluffy.

4 Crack the egg into the bowl. Beat the mixture well. Stir in the milk. Mix well.

Step 4

5 Hold the sifter over the mixing bowl. Measure the flour, baking powder, and salt into the sifter. Sift them into the mixing bowl.

Step 5

34

6 Stir gently, just enough to moisten the flour mixture. Then carefully stir the blueberries into the mixture.

7 Fill each muffin cup ⅔ full. Bake the muffins on the middle oven rack for 20 to 25 minutes.

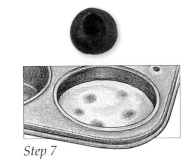

Step 7

8 Insert a toothpick into one of the muffins. If it comes out clean, the muffins are done.

9 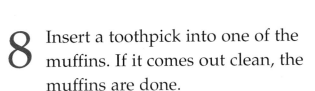 Have an adult remove the muffin pan from the oven. Let the muffins cool for a few minutes. Then arrange them in a basket or on a plate and serve them with butter and jam.

Saratoga Potatoes

Fried Saratoga potatoes add a crispy crunch to brunch.

Ingredients

- 4 large potatoes
- Cold water
- 8 ice cubes
- 2 cups shortening
- Salt

Equipment

- Vegetable peeler
- Large bowl
- Grater
- Paper towels
- Rubber spatula
- Measuring cup
- Large skillet
- Slotted spoon or skimmer
- Aluminum pie pan
- Serving plate

Serves 6

1 Have an adult help you peel the potatoes.

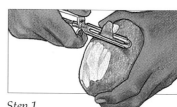

Step 1

2 Pour cold water into the bowl until it is half full. Then add the ice cubes.

3 Have an adult help you rub the potatoes over the wide slicer on the grater to cut them into very thin, round slices.

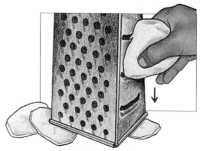

Step 3

4 As the potatoes are sliced, put them into the bowl of ice water to remove some of the starch.

5 Drain a handful of potato slices on the paper towels. Pat the tops with more paper towels. Drying the potatoes keeps the shortening from splattering when you put them into the skillet.

6 Have an adult help you fry the potatoes (steps 6 through 12). First, use the rubber spatula to add the shortening to the skillet. Melt the shortening over medium-high heat until it is very hot.

7 Use the slotted spoon or skimmer to put 1 potato slice into the shortening to test it. The shortening should bubble around the potato. If the potato turns brown quickly, the shortening is too hot—turn down the heat a little.

Step 7

8 Carefully move the rest of the dried slices from the paper towels into the hot shortening.

9 As the potatoes cook, separate any slices that stick together.

10 Fry the potatoes for 4 to 5 minutes, or until they turn a light golden color. Remove them from the skillet and lay them on paper towels to absorb the excess oil.

11 Put the hot slices into the pie pan and shake salt lightly over them. Then slide them onto the serving plate.

12 Fry the rest of the potatoes in the same way. If the shortening becomes too hot or smoky, turn down the heat.

Brunch Punch

Punch made with fresh fruit and bubbly soda water is a refreshing and thirst-quenching concoction.

Ingredients

- 3 lemons (to make ½ cup juice)
- 5 oranges (to make 2 cups juice)
- ½ cup sugar
- 1 cup water
- ¾ cup pineapple juice
- 2 cups chilled club soda
- Ice cubes
- Orange slices for garnish

Equipment

- Sharp knife
- Cutting board
- Juicer
- Strainer
- Pitcher
- Measuring cups
- Small saucepan
- Wooden spoon

Serves 8–10

1 ✋ Have an adult help you cut the lemons and oranges in half on the cutting board.

Step 1

2 Squeeze the juice out of the lemon and orange halves by turning them back and forth on the juicer while pushing down. Pour the juice through the strainer into the pitcher.

Step 2

3 Measure the sugar and water into the saucepan, and stir. Heat the mixture over medium-high heat until it *boils*, or bubbles rapidly, for 5 minutes.

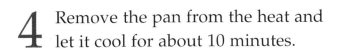

4 Remove the pan from the heat and let it cool for about 10 minutes.

5 ✋ Have an adult help you pour the sugar and water mixture into the pitcher. Then add the pineapple juice and stir well.

6 If you are not serving the punch right away, refrigerate the mixture until serving time. Just before serving the punch, measure 2 cups of cold club soda and pour it into the pitcher with the juice mixture. Stir gently to mix it all together.

7 Pour the punch into punch glasses. Add 2 or 3 ice cubes to each glass and garnish with a slice of fruit.

Drink to Your Health!

Victorians believed that soda water, or carbonated "fizzy" water, could improve their health. Drugstores featured **soda fountains,** *so customers could buy plain soda water and flavored sodas, like Coca-Cola and root beer, along with their medicines.*

39

Sunday Ham

A juicy ham slice was perfect for a proper brunch in 1904.

Ingredients

- 2-pound fully cooked ham slice
- 2 tablespoons water
- Parsley, curly lettuce, and lemon slices for garnish (optional)

Equipment

- Cutting board
- Sharp knife
- Skillet
- Measuring spoon
- Fork
- Serving plate

Serves 6

1 Place the ham slice on the cutting board. Have an adult help you trim away the fat from the edges. Cut the ham slice into serving-size pieces.

Step 1

2 Set the skillet on a stove burner. Measure the water into the skillet and turn the heat to medium high. Let the water get warm.

3 Put the ham pieces into the skillet and cook them about 3 minutes.

4 Turn over the pieces with a fork. Cook them for 3 more minutes. Then put the ham pieces onto a serving plate.

5 If you wish, arrange parsley sprigs and lettuce leaves around the plate and set 2 or 3 lemon slices on top of the ham.

Strawberries with Cream

Fresh strawberries and sweet cream are a simple but delicious combination.

ɪngredients

ɛ cups fresh
strawberries
ɪ pint heavy cream
ɪ cup sugar

ɛquipment

ᴘaring knife
ᴄolander
ᴘaper towels
ᴄutting board
ɪ small serving
ᴏwls or dishes
ᴄream pitcher
ᴍall sugar bowl

ᴇrves 6

1. Have an adult help you use the paring knife to remove the stem and leaves from each strawberry.

2. Put the strawberries into the colander and rinse them well under cold water. Drain them on paper towels.

3. Cut large berries into bite-size pieces. Put the berries into the serving bowls.

4. Pour cream into the cream pitcher. Put sugar in the sugar bowl. That way your guests can put the amount of cream and sugar they prefer on their strawberries.

Step 1

Cheesy Omelet

Melted cheese makes a creamy filling for this omelet.

Ingredients

- 6 eggs
- ½ teaspoon salt
- ⅛ teaspoon pepper
- 4 tablespoons water
- 2 tablespoons butter
- ½ cup grated cheese

Equipment

- Mixing bowl
- Fork
- Measuring cup and spoons
- Large skillet
- Spatula
- Serving dish

Serves 2–3

1 Crack the eggs into the mixing bowl. Use the fork to beat the eggs until they are well mixed.

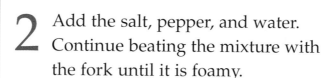
Step 1

2 Add the salt, pepper, and water. Continue beating the mixture with the fork until it is foamy.

3 Melt the butter in the skillet over medium-high heat until it is bubbly. Be careful not to let the butter burn.

4 Carefully pour the egg mixture into the skillet.

5 As the egg mixture cooks, use the spatula to push it gently toward the middle of the skillet. Have an adult help you tilt the pan slightly so the uncooked part of the mixture moves to the outside.

Step 5

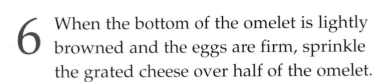

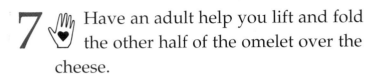

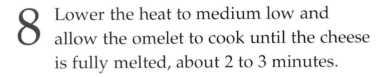

6 When the bottom of the omelet is lightly browned and the eggs are firm, sprinkle the grated cheese over half of the omelet.

Step 6

7 🤚 Have an adult help you lift and fold the other half of the omelet over the cheese.

Step 7

8 Lower the heat to medium low and allow the omelet to cook until the cheese is fully melted, about 2 to 3 minutes.

9 🤚 Have an adult help you slide the omelet out of the pan and onto the serving dish. Serve the omelet while it is hot.

Valentine's Day Fun

Saint Valentine's Day was one of Samantha's favorite holidays. She and Aunt Cornelia began making valentines weeks before the special day. They sat by the fire with their box of supplies and carefully pasted their valentines together. For some of her friends, Samantha made presents such as sweet-scented sachets and colorful trinket boxes. Samantha and Aunt Cornelia also baked heart-shaped cookies. They had fun decorating them with pretty valentine designs. When Valentine's Day arrived, Samantha had a party for her friends. She served them her sweet heart cookies, and everyone played parlor games like Pin the Heart on the Valentine!

Sweet Heart Cookies

Heart-shaped sugar cookies were a sweet valentine treat in Samantha's day. Here's an easy, modern version.

Ingredients

- 1 tube refrigerated sugar cookie dough
- 1 egg yolk
- ¼ teaspoon water
- Red food coloring

Equipment

- Rolling pin
- Heart-shaped cookie cutter
- Cookie sheet
- Small, unused artist's paintbrushes
- Spatula
- Wire rack

**Makes
24–30 cookies**

1 Preheat the oven to 350°. Prepare the dough according to the directions for rolled cookies.

2 Cut out heart shapes with the cookie cutter and place them on a cookie sheet.

3 Mix the egg yolk and water. Add 15 drops of red food coloring.

Valentine Queen

4 With the paint-brushes, paint valentine designs on the cookie dough.

5 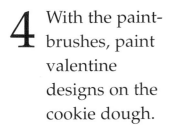 Bake the cook-ies for 7 to 10 minutes, or until golden. Have an adult take the pan from the oven. With the spatula, move the cookies to a wire rack to cool.

When Esther Howland received a fancy English valentine from an admirer in 1847, she was inspired to start the first American valentine company. She hired friends to help make the valentines around her parents' dining room table. Esther designed the cards. One worker made back-grounds, another cut out pictures to be glued on, a third added ribbon, and so on—just like an assembly line! Soon, Esther's New England Valentine Company was making thousands of dollars a year. And Esther was just 19 when she started her business!

Girls like Samantha loved to get valentines.

Victorian Valentines

Run your own valentine assembly line and make one-of-a-kind valentines!

Materials

- Newspaper
- Construction paper, old magazines, wrapping and tissue paper, paper lace or doilies, bits of ribbon and yarn, buttons, stickers
- Scissors
- White glue
- 2 or more friends—ask your friends to bring scissors and glue if you don't have enough

1 Cover a table with newspaper. Then arrange all your materials on the table.

2 Each guest makes a background card out of construction paper—anything from a folded card to a cutout shape.

Step 2

3 Each guest passes her background to the girl on her right. She adds one decoration of her choice to the background card she receives, then passes the valentine on again.

4 Keep passing the valentines around until everyone has added decorations.

Steps 3 & 4

5 The last girl in the assembly line might write a funny verse like this one:
   Roses are red, violets are blue,
   I'm glad I have a friend as great as you!

Apple Valentines

*Decorate shiny red apples
for simple, snappy
valentine gifts.*

Materials

- Ripe red apples
- Construction paper in pink, red, or white
- Scissors
- Pens or markers
- Hole punch
- Several 8-inch pieces of narrow ribbon, about ⅛ inch wide

1 Use the scissors to cut small heart shapes out of construction paper.

2 Write short valentine messages such as "I'm sweet on you!" on each one.

3 Punch a small hole in each heart, thread a ribbon through, and tie it to the stem of a bright red apple.

Tokens of Love

*In Samantha's time, people showed their affection by exchanging **tokens** such as letters, locks of hair, and small portraits. Some young ladies kept their tokens in heart-shaped silk pockets.*

Heart-Shaped Sachet

*Make a scented sachet
for someone special.*

Materials

- Pencil
- Sheet of tracing paper
- Scissors
- Straight pins
- Piece of cotton fabric, 5 inches square
- Piece of lace, 5 inches square
- Ruler
- Thread to match fabric
- Needle
- Spoon
- Potpourri
- 7-inch piece of ribbon, ⅛ inch wide

1 Use the pencil to trace the heart pattern shown on page 93 onto tracing paper. Then cut it out.

2 Pin the heart pattern onto the *wrong side,* or back side, of the fabric square. Then cut around the edge.

3 Unpin the pattern. Then cut out a heart from the lace in the same way.

4 Lay the fabric heart on the table with the *right side,* or front side, facing up.

5 Then lay the lace heart on top. Pin the edges of the two hearts together.

6 Cut an 18-inch piece of thread, and then thread the needle. Tie a double knot at one end of the thread.

Step 2

Step 5

7 Backstitch the hearts together, 1/4 inch from the edge. To backstitch, come up at A and then go down at B.

Step 7

8 Come up at C. Then go down at A and come up at D.

Step 8

9 Keep stitching until there are 2 inches left open. Then tie a knot close to your last stitch and cut off the extra thread.

Step 9

10 Unpin the fabric and turn it inside out. Spoon potpourri into the sachet until it's plump.

11 Tuck the raw edges of fabric inside the sachet. Pin the edges together and finish sewing them up.

Step 11

12 Remove the pins. For a finishing touch, tie a small ribbon bow and sew it to the top of the sachet.

A Sachet Keepsake

A bride like Aunt Cornelia might dry the flowers of her wedding bouquet and use the petals to make a sachet. Every time she smelled its sweet fragrance, she would recall her wedding day!

Trinket Box

*Fill this colorful box with
trinkets and treasures.*

Materials

- Sandpaper
- Unfinished wooden
  box with lid,
  3 by 4 inches
- 2 foam paintbrushes,
  each 1 inch wide
- Acrylic paint,
  any color
- Scissors
- Old magazines
  or greeting cards
- White glue
- Small bowl

1 Lightly sand the wooden box and lid.
Wipe away the dust. Use one of the
foam paintbrushes to paint the box and
lid inside and out.

2 Set both the box and lid aside to dry.
Keep the lid off the box. You'll need to
keep them separate until the very end
of this project.

3 Cut out small pictures from old
magazines and greeting cards. Make
sure your pictures are small enough
to fit on the box or its lid.

4 When you have cut out enough pictures,
think about how you'd like to arrange
them. For example, you might want
to put your favorite picture in the
center of the lid.

5 After you have planned your design, start gluing your pictures to the lid and the sides of the box. Make sure the pictures are glued on completely, with no edges curling up.

6 If any of the pictures stick out past the edges of the box or lid, trim them to fit.

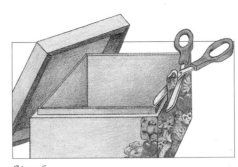

Step 6

7 Squeeze glue into the small bowl until it is about ¼ inch deep. Dip the other foam paintbrush in the glue.

8 Lightly brush a thin layer of glue over the lid and sides of the box. The glue will look milky at first, but it will dry clear. If the glue gets too thick, add a little water to thin it.

9 Let the glue dry for about 15 minutes. Then give the box and lid another coat of glue. When the glue is dry, your box is finished!

Scrap Pictures

*Victorian girls cut out bits of paper called **scrap** to decorate valentines, scrapbooks, boxes, and vases. Scrap often showed pictures of children, angels, hearts, or flowers. Some scrap even held little poems written in fancy script.*

February Fun

On frosty afternoons, Samantha and her friends loved to go ice-skating. Afterward, they gathered in Samantha's parlor to warm up with hot cocoa and cookies. Then they were ready to play valentine games like these!

I Sent My Love a Valentine

All you need for this game is an envelope. Choose one player to be the Dropper, and have the others sit in a circle. The Dropper takes the envelope and skips around the outside of the circle while the others sing this song to the tune of Yankee Doodle:

> *I sent my love a valentine*
> *And on the way I dropped it.*
> *Another love just picked it up*
> *And put it in her pocket.*

At the end of the song, the Dropper drops the envelope behind one of the girls. That player picks up the envelope. Then both the Dropper and the girl with the envelope run around the circle in opposite directions until one of them reaches the empty space in the circle and sits down. The player who is left without a seat becomes the next Dropper.

Valentine Queen

Hide valentines around the room. The person who finds the most is the Valentine Queen!

Pin the Heart on the Valentine

Cut out a large cardboard heart with a circle drawn in the center. Fasten the heart onto a wall. Give each player a little red heart with a piece of double-sided tape stuck on the back. Blindfold each player and have her try to "pin" the little heart inside the circle on the big heart. The player who comes closest to the circle wins.

A Piney Point Adventure

To Samantha, Grandmary's summer home in the mountains was the most magical place in the world. From the early-morning mist that rose off the lake to the twinkling lights of the fireflies at dusk, Piney Point was a world of mystery and wonder.

Days at Piney Point were active ones. Rain or shine, Samantha and her friends Agnes and Agatha never ran short of things to do. On rainy days, there were wildflowers to press, seashells to collect, and mountain scenery to paint. On sunny days, there were trips to the meadow and cool afternoon splashes in the lake. And in the fall, there were leaves and nuts to gather. There was always something to do at Piney Point!

Paint an Impression

Capture nature's beauty with quick dabs and dashes of paint—just as famous artists did in Samantha's time.

Materials

- Magnifying glass
- White sketch paper
- Pencil
- Artist's paintbrush
- Tempera paint, watercolors, or pastels such as Cray-pas®
- Easel or stool

1 Look closely at the detail of the painting on page 59. Notice that the flowers are made with short, quick strokes and dots of paint.

2 Collect your materials.

3 Impressionists often painted outdoors. Set up your easel outdoors, or sit on the stool with your paper on your lap.

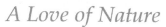

A Love of Nature

In Victorian times, girls and women rambled the countryside to hunt for butterflies and pick wildflowers that bloomed in the meadows. Nature was something Victorians looked at and enjoyed. They painted scenery, studied wild plants and animals, and kept albums of pressed leaves and wildflowers.

Painting Outdoors

Turn-of-the-century artists called **Impressionists** painted pictures in a bold new way. They wanted to paint people in informal settings, and many Impressionists enjoyed painting outdoors. They used broad strokes and dabs of bright color to show their impressions of how things looked in the natural light.

At first, people thought the paintings looked messy. Many Impressionist painters had a hard time selling their paintings. Today, these paintings are worth millions of dollars, and Impressionism is one of the best-loved art styles in the world.

4 Lightly sketch the outlines of your picture.

5 Now fill in your picture with dabs and dashes of paint.

A paint box from the turn of the century

*In this painting, **The Artist's Garden at Giverny,** Claude Monet (mo-NAY) created the impression of flowers and trees with quick strokes of bright color.*

Seashell Picture Frame

Use pretty seashells to frame a favorite photo.

Materials

- Pencil
- Ruler
- 3 pieces of cardboard, each 6½ inches square
- Scissors
- Foam paintbrush, 1 inch wide
- Acrylic paints, any colors
- Seashells (available in craft stores, or collect your own by a lake or ocean)
- Craft glue
- 1 picture, 4 inches square
- 1 piece of cardboard, 3½ by 5 inches

1 Use the pencil and ruler to draw a line along each edge of one of the cardboard squares, 1½ inches from each edge.

2 Ask an adult to help you poke the scissors through the square in the middle of the cardboard. Then cut out the square.

3 Use the pencil and ruler to draw a line along each edge of a second square of cardboard, 1¼ inches from each edge.

4 Ask an adult to help you poke the scissors through the square in the middle of the cardboard. Then cut out the square.

5 Paint each frame piece on 1 side. Let the paint dry, and then paint the other side of each frame piece. Paint the edges, too.

1½ inches

Step 1

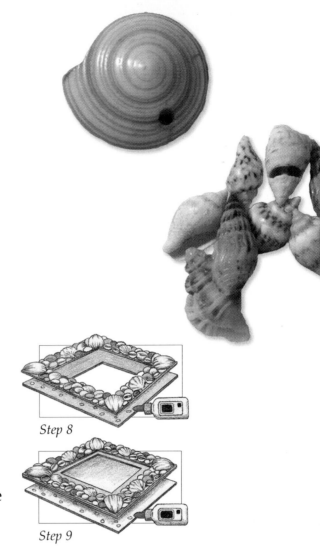

6 Lay the frame piece with the larger opening on a table.

7 Plan your shell design. For example, you might want to place the prettiest shell at the top of your frame. When you're happy with your design, glue the shells to the frame piece.

8 Lay the other frame piece on the table. Dot glue along all 4 outer edges. Place the shell frame on top of the glue. Make sure the edges are lined up.

Step 8

9 Lay the third cardboard square on the table. Dot glue along 3 edges. Place the frame on top of the glue. Again, make sure the edges are lined up.

Step 9

10 When the glue has dried, slide your picture into the frame.

11 To make a stand for your frame, fold the cardboard rectangle in half. Then glue it to the back of the frame as shown.

Step 11

Pressed-Flower Bookmark

Pressed flowers make beautiful bookmarks for your family and friends.

Materials

- Small, fresh-picked flowers
- 2 sheets of white paper
- 4 or 5 heavy books
- Piece of parchment paper, 2 by 6 inches
- White glue
- Small bowl
- Foam paintbrush, 1 inch wide
- Piece of poster board, 2 by 6 inches
- Small artist's paintbrush
- Paper lace cut from doilies
- Piece of satin cord, 8 inches long

1 Arrange your flowers on a sheet of white paper.

2 Cover the flowers with another piece of paper, and then slip them between the pages of a heavy book. Stack 3 or 4 more heavy books on top to add weight.

3 Press the flowers for about a week. Check them every few days. If the paper gets moist, replace it with new paper.

4 When the flowers are dry, plan your design. Arrange the flowers on the parchment paper to make sure they fit.

5 When you're happy with your arrangement, remove the flowers. Squeeze a little glue into the small bowl.

6 Dip the foam paintbrush into the glue, and then brush a thin layer of glue onto the poster board. If the glue is too thick, thin it with a little water.

Steps 6, 7

7 Place the parchment paper on top, making sure the edges are lined up. Smooth out any air bubbles.

8 Glue the flowers onto the parchment paper. Be careful not to crush the petals.

9 Use the artist's paintbrush to lightly brush a thin coat of glue over the flowers. The glue will look milky at first, but it will dry clear.

10 When the glue is dry, use the foam brush to coat the front of the bookmark with glue.

11 For a finishing touch, trim your bookmark with paper lace and tie on a satin cord.

THE LANGUAGE OF FLOWERS

In Victorian times, each kind of flower had a special meaning. If a young lady received a bouquet from an admirer, she carefully studied the kinds of flowers in the arrangement to find out exactly how the young man felt about her!

Pansy
Thoughtfulness

Daisy
Beauty

Red Rose
Love

Blue Violet
Faithfulness

Forget-Me-Not
True love

Primrose
Confidence

Honeysuckle
Generosity

Geranium
True friendship

Soap Bubbles

Mix up a big bowl of bubbles and have a bubble party!

Materials

- 1 cup water
- ¾ cup liquid dish soap, such as Palmolive®
- Small saucepan
- 10-inch piece of copper wire, 22 gauge
- Scissors
- Small bowl

1 Pour the water and dish soap into the saucepan.

2 Ask an adult to help you heat the mixture over medium-high heat until it *boils*, or bubbles rapidly. Then turn off the heat.

3 While the mixture cools, make a bubble wand from the copper wire. Bend one end of the wire into a circle about 1½ inches wide.

  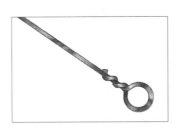 

4 Twist the circle closed, and then cut off the short tail of wire.

5 Bend the other end of the wire into a circle about $1/2$ inch wide in the same way.

6 Ask an adult to help you pour the bubble mixture into the small bowl.

7 Dip either end of the wand into the bubble mixture, and start blowing bubbles!

Make a Bug Collection

Samantha always took her butterfly net and magnifying glass when she went exploring on Teardrop Island.

Materials

- Clean, empty glass jar with lid
- Insects, caterpillars, butterflies, or spiders with part of their natural habitat
- Encyclopedia or insect book
- Drawing paper
- Pencil
- Colored pencils

1 Have an adult help you punch some holes in the lid of the jar.

2 Collect insects, caterpillars, butterflies, or spiders in the jar. Be sure to include part of the bugs' natural habitat, so they have things to eat and crawl on.

3 Use an encyclopedia or insect book to identify your specimens.

A Craze for Collecting

A fossilized insect

4 Draw a picture of each bug and label it. Once you've finished your drawings, let the bugs go. Then you can collect new specimens.

In Samantha's day, collecting was all the rage. People kept special display cases in their homes to show off their collections of natural objects such as butterflies, birds' nests, seashells, rocks, and mosses. Magazines even encouraged housewives to stuff dead birds and animals and mount them in the parlor in lifelike poses! People were also eager to collect and display the fossilized remains of extinct plants and animals.

*Fossils of a sea animal called a **trilobite** (TRY-la-bite); a leaf; and a spiral-shelled **ammonite** (AM-a-nite)*

Glass Paperweight

Set your glass paperweight on a table or shelf where it will catch the light.

Materials

- Small glass bowl, jar, or votive candle-holder
- Piece of poster board, 5 inches square
- Black marker or pen
- Scissors
- Piece of felt, 5 inches square
- Fabric glue
- Small objects, such as dried flowers, stones, shells, pinecones, or toys
- Piece of satin cord, 12 inches long

1 Place the glass container upside down on the poster board.

2 Use the marker or pen to trace around the container. Cut out the outline.

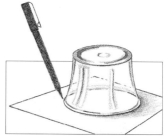

Step 2

3 Place the poster board outline on the felt square. Use the black marker or pen to trace around the poster board, and then cut out the felt.

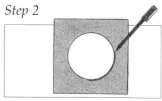

Step 3

4 Dot glue around the edges of the poster board. Then glue the felt to the poster board. Make sure the edges of the felt and poster board are lined up.

Step 4

5 Decide what you'd like to put inside your paperweight. You may want to use one object, or an arrangement of several objects.

6 When you're happy with your arrangement, place the glass container over it to make sure everything fits.

7 Remove the glass container. Glue your object or objects to the felt. Let the glue dry for a few minutes.

8 Squeeze small dots of glue around the edges of the felt. Place the glass container upside down onto the glue. Make sure the edges of the container line up with the edges of the felt.

Step 8

Step 9

9 Glue the satin cord around the bottom edge of your paperweight. Cut off any extra cord.

10 When the glue is dry, your paperweight is complete!

Collections Under Glass

In the early 1900s, girls and women sometimes arranged their family's collection of natural objects into a fanciful composition and displayed it under a glass dome called a **shade.**

Leaf-Print Wrapping Paper

Wrap presents in paper you've printed yourself!

Materials

- Fresh-picked leaves with stems, any sizes
- Newspaper
- Sheet of white drawing paper
- Piece of cardboard, 4 inches square
- Acrylic paints, any colors
- Small bowls
- Small sponges
- Sheet of craft paper, 11 by 17 inches

1 Lay the leaves on a sheet of newspaper, with the raised veins facing up. Place the drawing paper and the cardboard square next to the newspaper.

Step 1

2 To practice making a leaf print, pour a little paint into a small bowl, and then dip a sponge into the paint.

3 Hold one of the leaves by its stem. Gently dab paint onto the leaf.

Step 3

4 Pick up the leaf by its stem and place it on the sheet of white paper, painted side down.

5 Place the cardboard square on top of the leaf and press down. Hold it for a few seconds, and then remove it.

6 Carefully peel away the leaf by its stem. You've made a leaf print!

Step 6

7 Practice a few more times with different leaves. Try different paint colors. Use a new sponge for each color, and don't mix colors.

8 When you're happy with your practice leaf prints, you're ready to make leaf-print wrapping paper. Spread the craft paper next to the newspaper.

9 Plan your design. For example, you might want to print the largest leaf in the middle of the paper and print smaller leaves around it.

10 Make leaf prints on the craft paper just as you've practiced.

11 When you've finished printing your design, let the paint dry for about an hour. Then your wrapping paper is ready to use.

Botany Class

Botany, *or the study of plant life, was part of a good education for many American children in Samantha's time. Teachers took their students out into fields to collect samples of plants and flowers to study in the classroom.*

71

Nut Crunch Apples

These healthy treats make a great snack or dessert—and they'll fill your kitchen with a wonderful spicy smell as they simmer!

Ingredients

- 4 medium cooking apples
- 4 tablespoons currants
- 4 tablespoons walnuts, chopped
- 2 tablespoons brown sugar
- 2 tablespoons butter, softened
- 2 cups apple juice
- Cinnamon (optional)

Equipment

- Paring knife
- Melon baller or small spoon
- Small bowl
- Measuring spoons
- Mixing spoon
- Skillet with cover
- Measuring cup

Serves 4

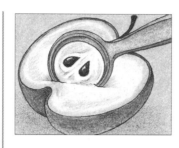

1 Cut the apples in half with the knife. Have an adult help you remove the apple cores with the melon baller or small spoon.

2 In the small bowl, mix together the currants, walnuts, brown sugar, and softened butter.

3 Spoon the mixture into the apple halves. Place the apple halves in the skillet, stuffed sides up.

4 Add the apple juice to the skillet. Cover and simmer the apples for 15 minutes, or until they are tender.

5 Spoon some of the juice over the apples when you serve them. Try sprinkling your apple with a touch of cinnamon!

Little Brown Squirrel

Families in Samantha's time sometimes had nut-gathering contests. The person who filled her basket first was the Little Brown Squirrel, the person who had the largest variety of nuts was the Little Red Squirrel, and everyone else was a Little Gray Squirrel. After the contest, most of the nuts were left outside for the real squirrels to enjoy.

Piney Point Games

In the summer, well-to-do families like Samantha's escaped the heat by moving to homes near the ocean or in the mountains. At Grandmary's summer home, Piney Point, life was less formal, and Samantha could play outside to her heart's content. You can enjoy some of the same outdoor games today!

Hoop and Stick

First, make the hoop and the stick. Use a 14-inch wooden hoop (the inner ring of an embroidery hoop works well) and a 2-foot wooden dowel that is $3/8$ inch wide. Paint a base coat on the hoop and the stick. Let dry, then paint designs on the hoop and stick if you like. To play, hold the stick in one hand and the hoop in the other. Roll the hoop with your hand to start it. Run along beside the hoop, and keep it rolling by pushing it with the stick. It takes practice!

Plum Pudding

Try this Hopscotch pattern:

1 Use chalk to draw the Hopscotch pattern on the sidewalk or driveway. The top of the pattern is called the Plum Pudding. Begin by standing at the star.

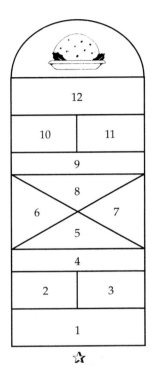

2 Toss a stone into square 1. Hop into the square on one foot. With your free foot, kick the stone out near the star. Then hop back out, still on one foot.

3 Toss the stone into square 2. Hop to square 1 and then to square 2. Kick the stone to square 1 and then hop back to square 1. Then kick the stone out near the star. Hop back out. If you or your stone lands in the wrong square or you step on a line, you lose your turn. On your next turn, start again with the last square you completed successfully.

4 Hop the rest of the pattern this way. When your stone is in square 8, you can rest both feet on squares 6 and 7. But you must hop on one foot into square 8 before you kick the stone out to square 7.

5 When you reach the Plum Pudding, you must kick the stone hard enough to send it all the way to the star with one kick. The first player to do this wins!

Hopscotch

Children all over the world have played Hopscotch for hundreds of years. By the turn of the century, immigrants from many lands had brought different Hopscotch patterns with them to America.

By the Fireside

On winter evenings, Samantha and Grandmary spent time together in the parlor. They warmed themselves beside the cheery fire Mr. Hawkins made. Grandmary read by the light of a gas lamp while Samantha cut out lacy paper snowflakes or practiced her sewing and fancy embroidery. Sometimes Mrs. Hawkins brought out one of Samantha's favorite treats— gingerbread fresh from the oven.

If Samantha and Grandmary had company, they might "have a sing" around the piano or play parlor games like charades and Twine the Garland. Samantha also loved to make silhouettes to add to her scrapbook. Uncle Gard was her favorite subject. He always made the funniest faces!

Silhouettes

Before families had their own cameras, people often captured a loved one's likeness in a silhouette. Snip a silhouette of one of your friends!

Materials

- Chair
- Desk lamp
- Table
- Masking tape
- 2 sheets of white paper, each 11 by 14 inches
- Pencil
- Scissors
- Sheet of black paper, 11 by 14 inches
- White crayon or piece of white chalk
- Glue

1 Place the chair sideways about 1 foot from a blank wall.

2 Place the lamp on a table about 5 feet from the chair. Shine the lamp onto the wall.

3 Seat a friend or family member in the chair. You should see your subject's shadow on the wall.

4 Tape a sheet of white paper to the wall so it catches your subject's shadow. You may need to move your subject or the lamp until the shadow fits onto the sheet of paper.

5 When the shadow fits on the paper, use a pencil to trace the outline carefully. Make sure your subject sits very still!

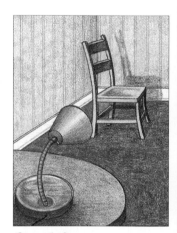

Steps 1, 2

Step 4

6 After you've finished the outline, untape the paper from the wall.

7 Cut out the outline. Then lay it on top of the sheet of black paper.

8 Use the white crayon or piece of white chalk to trace around your subject's outline.

9 Carefully cut out the outline. You've made a silhouette!

10 Glue the silhouette onto the other sheet of white paper. Frame it and hang it on the wall, or start a silhouette scrapbook.

Step 8

Photography

*Early cameras, like the one shown at right, were bulky and complicated. But in 1900, Kodak Company produced the **Brownie,** the first camera made especially for children. It cost one dollar. For the first time, children could take pictures of family members and friends with their own cameras.*

Ice Cream Snowballs

Roll vanilla ice cream in coconut for a cool and crunchy treat.

Ingredients

- 2 cups shredded coconut
- 1 quart vanilla ice cream, softened
- 12 ladyfinger cookies

Equipment

- Measuring cup
- Shallow bowl
- Ice cream scoop
- 2 large spoons
- Freezer container with lid

Serves 6

1 Put the coconut into the bowl. Scoop out a large ball of ice cream, drop it into the coconut, and, using the spoons, roll it around until it is covered.

Step 1

2 Lift out the ice cream snowball and put it into the freezer container.

3 Repeat Steps 1 and 2 until you have 6 ice cream snowballs. Keep the snowballs separated.

4 Cover the container tightly and freeze the snowballs for at least 2 hours.

5 Take the container out of the freezer 15 minutes before you are ready to serve dessert. This allows the ice cream snowballs to soften a little, so they will be easy to eat with a spoon.

6 Put each ice cream snowball in a pretty dish, and serve with 2 ladyfinger cookies.

Coconut

In 1895, Franklin Baker of Philadelphia discovered a way to preserve coconut meat. Baker's shredded coconut quickly became popular for home cooking.

Vanilla

Vanilla extract is another product that became available when Samantha was a girl. Before that, Americans most often flavored desserts with lemons, which were common and inexpensive.

Frozen Dainties

Ice cream was the national dessert in 1904, just as it is today. People of all ages flocked to ice cream parlors for sundaes and flavored ice cream, including Samantha's favorite—peppermint. Children could also buy ice cream and ices from *hokey-pokey men,* street vendors who sold inexpensive frozen *dainties.* In Samantha's time, a dainty meant a small treat.

Toss Pillow

Tasseled toss pillows dressed up Samantha's parlor. They'll look great in your living room or bedroom, too!

Materials

- 2 pieces of fabric, each 12 inches square
- Straight pins
- Scissors
- Ruler
- Thread to match fabric
- Needle
- Polyester stuffing
- 4 tassels

1 Lay 1 piece of fabric on a table with the *right side*, or front side, facing up.

2 Place the other piece of fabric on top, with the *wrong side*, or back side, facing up. Pin the squares together along 3 sides.

3 Cut an 18-inch piece of thread, and then thread the needle. Tie a double knot at one end of the thread.

4 Sew running stitches along the 3 pinned sides, 1/4 inch from the edge. To make running stitches, come up at A and go down at B.

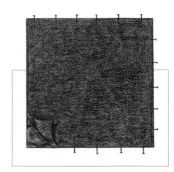

Step 2

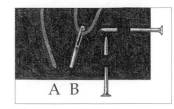

Step 4

5 Come up at C and go down at D. Continue stitching this way. When you finish stitching, tie a knot close to your last stitch and cut off the extra thread.

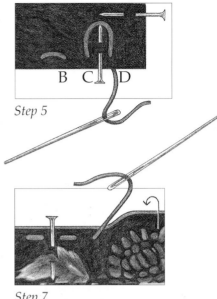

Step 5

6 Unpin the fabric and turn the pillow right side out. Fill the pillow with stuffing until it's plump.

7 Then fold in the last edges of the pillow and pin them together. Sew the pillow closed.

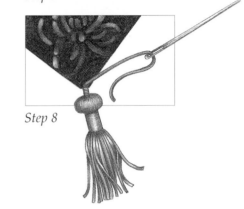

Step 7

8 Remove the pins. Finish your toss pillow by sewing colorful tassels onto the corners.

Step 8

Candy Crystals

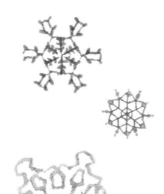

These sparkling candy crystals grow like magic!

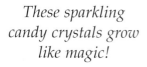

Ingredients

- 1 cup water
- 3 cups white sugar

Equipment

- Small saucepan
- Wooden spoon
- 3 drinking glasses
- Food coloring (optional)
- 3 cotton cords, each 10 inches long
- 3 pencils
- Small plate

1 Pour the water and 2 cups of sugar into the saucepan. Have an adult help you heat the sugar water over medium-high heat until it *boils,* or bubbles rapidly. Stir until the sugar dissolves. The water will be clear.

2 Have an adult help you add the remaining sugar a little at a time until it won't dissolve anymore. You may not need to use all the sugar you measured out. Turn off the heat.

3 Let the sugar water cool for 15 minutes. Carefully pour the sugar water into the glasses. Mix in food coloring if you like.

4 Tie one end of each cotton cord around each pencil. Then lay the pencils across the tops of the glasses. Let the cords hang down into the sugar water.

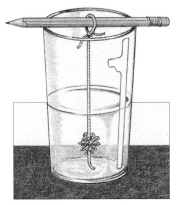

Step 4

5 In a day or so, candy crystals will form on the cords. Lift the cords out of the glasses and let the crystals harden on the plate. Enjoy!

The Snowflake Man

*In 1885, Wilson Bently took the first photograph of a snowflake through a microscope. Over the next 50 years, he took more than 4,500 **photo-micrographs**, which are still used to study snowflakes today.*

Gingerbread

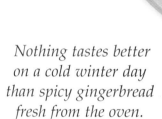

Ingredients

- Butter to grease baking dish
- ¼ cup butter
- 1 egg
- ½ cup buttermilk
- ½ cup light molasses
- 1½ cups flour
- ¼ cup sugar
- ¼ teaspoon baking soda
- 1 teaspoon baking powder
- ¼ teaspoon salt
- ¼ teaspoon ground cloves
- 2 teaspoons ground ginger
- 1 teaspoon cinnamon
- Powdered sugar or whipped cream (optional)

Equipment

- 8-inch square baking dish
- Measuring cups and spoons
- Small saucepan
- Medium mixing bowl
- Wire whisk
- Large mixing bowl
- Fork
- Mixing spoon
- Toothpick
- Pot holders

Serves 6–8

Nothing tastes better on a cold winter day than spicy gingerbread fresh from the oven.

1 Preheat the oven to 350°. Grease the baking dish with butter.

2 Have an adult help you melt ¼ cup butter in the saucepan over low heat. Be careful not to let the butter burn. Then turn off the heat and let the butter cool.

3 Crack the egg into the medium mixing bowl. Beat the egg with a wire whisk.

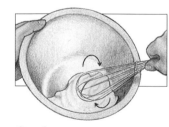

Step 3

4 Add the buttermilk, molasses, and melted butter to the egg. Mix well.

5 Measure the flour, sugar, baking soda, baking powder, salt, cloves, ginger, and cinnamon into the large mixing bowl. Mix them together using the fork.

6 Pour the liquid ingredients into the flour mixture. Stir to make a smooth batter.

7 Pour the batter into the baking dish. Bake the gingerbread on the center rack of the oven for 25 to 30 minutes.

8 Check to see if the gingerbread is done by inserting a toothpick into the center. If the toothpick comes out clean, the gingerbread is done.

9  Have an adult take the gingerbread out of the oven. Let it sit for about 5 minutes to serve it warm. Or let the gingerbread cool to room temperature.

10 Cut the gingerbread. Serve it with powdered sugar or whipped cream.

Cinnamon

Cloves

The spices that flavor gingerbread come from the bark, flower buds, and roots of tropical trees and plants. In Samantha's day, some people used ginger as a medicine to cure stomachaches and colds.

Ginger

Gingerbread Houses

At Christmas time, children like Samantha loved to help build houses out of hard gingerbread. They used gumdrops, sugar wafers, caramel squares, and honey sticks for decorations.

Fireside Games

In Samantha's time, people gathered by the parlor fireplace to spend sociable hours with family and friends. Girls played tea party and circle games. Young and old enjoyed word games and charades. You can play parlor games just as Samantha did— even if you don't have a parlor!

Twine the Garland

In this parlor game from Samantha's time, girls pretended that they were the garlands that decorated their fireplace mantels.

1 All the players hold hands and form a circle.

2 Without letting go of each others' hands, begin to twist under your arms and around each other.

3 Twist until you form a tight knot. While you twist, sing, "Twine the garland, girls!"

4 Then untwist and sing, "Untwine the garland, girls!"

I Am a Gold Lock

This silly word game always got Samantha giggling. Tell your friends to repeat everything you say, except they should say the word *key* where you say the word *lock*.

You: I am a gold lock
Friends: I am a gold key.
You: I am a silver lock.
Friends: I am a silver key.
You: I am a brass lock.
Friends: I am a brass key.
You: I am a monk lock.
Friends: I am a monk-key!

Get Shocked!

Electric power was first supplied to homes in Samantha's time. "Playing Electricity" was a game Samantha loved! Join hands in a circle around the person who is "It." That person covers her eyes. Then one player announces, "I'm turning the lights on!" and sends an imaginary "electric shock" around the circle by squeezing the hand of a player next to her, who squeezes the hand of the player next to her, and so on. "It" opens her eyes and tries to spot the shock as it travels around the circle. If she catches someone squeezing, that player becomes It.

These young ladies from 1909 are portraying the Pilgrims' farewell to the "Mayflower."

Tableaux Vivants
(tab-LOH vee-VAHN)

Tableaux vivants means "living pictures" in French. Players divide into 2 teams. Team A poses as a famous painting or sculpture, or as a scene from a book or historical event. Team A lets Team B know if they are posing from a painting, sculpture, book, or event. Team B tries to guess what they are. When Team B guesses correctly, it's their turn to pose.

Want to Know More?

Here are some fun ways you and your friends can get an inside view of life when the twentieth century was brand-new!

Read Books Set in Samantha's Time

- *Phoebe's Revolt*
  by Natalie Babbitt

- *Don't You Dare Shoot That Bear!*
  by Robert Quackenbush

- *Fire! The Beginnings of the Labor Movement*
  by Barbara Diamond Goldin

- *The Bells of Christmas*
  by Virginia Hamilton

- *I Go with My Family to Grandma's*
  by Riki Levinson

- *Our Century: 1900–1910*
  by Janice Greene

- *Ida B. Wells-Barnett: A Voice Against Violence*
  by Patricia and Fredrick McKissack

- *Hattie and the Wild Waves*
  by Barbara Cooney

Victrolas brought music into turn-of-the-century parlors.

Listen to Music of the Early 1900s

- *La Mer*
  by Claude Debussy

- *Madama Butterfly*
  by Giacomo Puccini

- "Maple Leaf Rag"
  by Scott Joplin

- "Yankee Doodle Boy"
  by George M. Cohan

Watch Movies Set in Samantha's Time

- *A Little Princess*
- *Mary Poppins*
- *Meet Me in St. Louis*
- *Peter Pan*
- *Pollyanna*
- *The Unsinkable Molly Brown*

Visit Museums About Samantha's Era

- Tuskegee Institute National Historic
  Site, Carver Museum
  1212 Old Montgomery Rd.
  Tuskegee Institute, Alabama 36088
  *Includes the restored home of African
  American educator Booker T. Washington*

- Susan B. Anthony House
  17 Madison St.
  Rochester, New York 14608
  The birthplace of the famous suffragist

- Henry Ford Museum & Greenfield Village
  20900 Oakwood Blvd.
  Dearborn, Michigan 48124
  *Includes a re-created American village and
  a museum of inventions*

- Jane Addams's Hull House Museum
  800 South Halsted St.
  Chicago, Illinois 60607
  Jane Addams's settlement house

Jane Addams started Hull House to help immigrants in Chicago.

Flower Basket

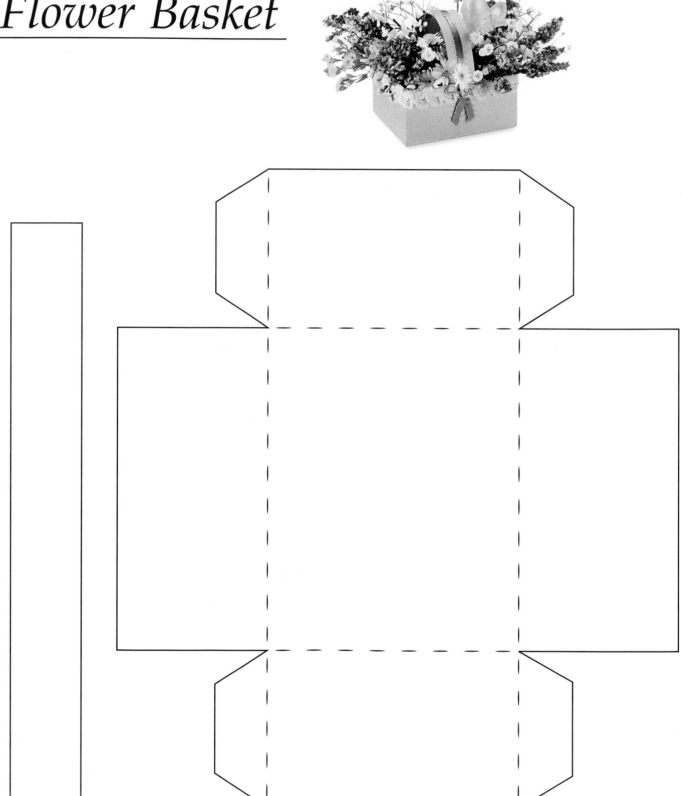

Sachet Heart

Visit our Web site at **americangirl.com**

02 03 04 05 06 07 08 09 QWD 10 9 8 7 6 5 4 3 2 1

Questions or comments?
Call 1-800-845-0005 or write to
Customer Service, Pleasant Company, 8400 Fairway Place, Middleton, WI 53562.

PICTURE CREDITS

Page 8—servants, Wisconsin Historical Society WHi (V22) 1387; p. 9—Queen Victoria, Royal Collection Enterprises, Ltd., Windsor, U.K. (896N/95); p. 13—girl in hairbow, Collection of Thomas H. Gandy and Joan W. Gandy; p. 17—women on veranda, Bettmann/CORBIS; p. 19—*Miss Mary Ellison,* by Mary Cassatt, Chester Dale Collection, photograph © Board of Trustees, National Gallery of Art, Washington; p. 27—iceman, Wisconsin Historical Society WHi (VS) 2775; p. 33—table-setting lesson, Wisconsin Historical Society WHi (D487) 426; p. 39—soda fountain, Bettmann/CORBIS; p. 47—valentines, Roberta Etter Photographs; p. 59—paint set, Robert Opie Collection; *The Artist's Garden at Giverny,* by Claude Monet, © Archivo Iconografico, S.A./CORBIS; pp. 60–61—family photos courtesy of the Klipsch, Rieder, and Ross families; pp. 66-67—butterflies, © Index Stock Imagery, Inc.; fossils courtesy of Gerald Gunderson; p. 69—collection under glass, Henry Ford Museum, Greenfield Village; p. 71—botany class, Culver Pictures; p. 73—nutting party, Library of Congress; p. 75—girls playing Hopscotch, Bettmann/CORBIS; p. 79—photographer, Missouri Historical Society, St. Louis, MO (LPE 0181A); p. 81—vanilla label, The Strong Museum, Rochester, NY; hokey-pokey man, Bettmann/CORBIS; p. 85—snowflake man, Jericho VT Historical Society; p. 88—tea party, Library of Congress, courtesy Mrs. Sharp's Traditions Collection of Antique Images; p. 89—tableaux vivants, *Harpers Bazaar,* 1909; p. 90—book cover from *Hattie and the Wild Waves* by Barbara Cooney, copyright © 1990 by Barbara Cooney. Used by permission of Viking Penguin, an imprint of Penguin Putnam Books for Young Readers, a division of Penguin Putnam Inc.; p. 91—Victrola, Christie's Images; Hull House, University of Illinois at Chicago, The University Library, Jane Addams Memorial Collection; Jane Addams, Smith College, Sophia Smith Collection, photo by Cox, Chicago, IL n.d.(SRA3).

Written by Tamara England, Michelle Jones, and Peg Ross
Cover illustration by Dan Andreasen
Interior illustrations by Dan Andreasen and Ann Boyajian
Step-by-step illustrations by Susan McAliley and Geri Strigenz-Bourget
Photography by Mark Salisbury, Kevin White, and Jamie Young
Edited by Tamara England and Peg Ross
Designed and art directed by Lara Klipsch Elliott, Ingrid Slamer, and Jane Varda
Produced by Paula Moon and Richmond Powers
Historical research by Sally Wood

Library of Congress Cataloging-in-Publication Data

Samantha's friendship fun./ [written by Tamara England, Michelle Jones, and Peg Ross; cover illustration by Dan Andreasen, interior illustrations by Dan Andreasen and Ann Boyajian].
p. cm.
Summary: Crafts, recipes, and games are designed to give a sense of the early 1900s, or the period setting for books in the American Girls collection which feature the character named Samantha.
ISBN 1-58485-587-8
1. Handicraft for Girls—United States—Juvenile literature. 2. Cookery, American—Juvenile literature. 3. United States—Social life and customs—20th century—Juvenile literature. [1. Handicraft. 2. Cookery, American. 3. United States—Social life and customs—20th century.] I. England, Tamara. II. Jones, Michelle. III. Ross, Peg. IV. Andreasen, Dan, ill. V. Boyajian, Ann, ill.
TT171 .S2623 2002
745.5—dc21   2002018218

**Special thanks to the children who tested
the crafts and recipes in this book and
gave us their valuable comments:**

Nicole Anderson, Stephanie Auen, Emily Ballweg,
Amelia Barber, Meredith Barbera, Julia Barton,
Jessica Baumgarten, Samantha Bechmann, Michelle Bridge,
Alisa Brown, Katie Bush, Ashleigh Conrad, Cassie Dabel,
Emily Dresen, Hannah Flake, Carla Gilbertson,
Emily Giovanni, Samantha Golden, Allison Guilfoil,
Lauren Hackbarth, Emily Hauschen, Elizabeth Heymann,
Emily Holler, Katherine Huber, Shannon Johnson,
Kari Jordan, Amanda Keller, Michael Kittle,
Meagan Lowenberg, Marianna March, Mallory Mason,
Mary Minahan, Emily Morrison, Meghan Moyer,
Clara Neale, Meredith Newlin, Saree Olkes,
Chelsea Osterby, Sophia Ott, Kati Peiss, Sarah Peterson,
Megan Petrie, Lindsay Polasek, Christina Quale,
Terra Randall, Clarlie Rasmussen, Lauren Roberts,
Diana Rodriguez, Meghan Rohde, Mollie Rostad,
Monica Saidler, Dawn Schwartz, Jessa Sharkey,
Jennifer Sharpe, Elizabeth Skogen, Elizabeth Solberg,
Carly Sorenson, Ashley Strassman, Rachel Tham,
Vanessa Theis, Rebecca Theisen, Heather Thue,
Heidi Tiefenthaler, Ashley and Lindsey Trachtenberg,
Jennifer Tuggle, Sarah Verrill, Caitlin Wichlacz,
and Nick Young

THE BOOKS ABOUT SAMANTHA

MEET SAMANTHA • An American Girl
Samantha becomes good friends with Nellie, a servant girl,
and together they plan a secret midnight adventure.

SAMANTHA LEARNS A LESSON • A School Story
Samantha becomes Nellie's teacher, but Nellie has some
very important lessons to teach Samantha, too.

SAMANTHA'S SURPRISE • A Christmas Story
Uncle Gard's friend Cornelia is ruining Samantha's
Christmas. But Christmas morning brings surprises!

HAPPY BIRTHDAY, SAMANTHA! • A Springtime Story
When Eddie Ryland spoils Samantha's birthday party,
Cornelia's twin sisters know just what to do.

SAMANTHA SAVES THE DAY • A Summer Story
Samantha enjoys a peaceful summer at Piney Point, until
a terrible storm strands her on Teardrop Island!

CHANGES FOR SAMANTHA • A Winter Story
When Samantha finds out that Nellie is living in an
orphanage, she must think of a way to help her escape.

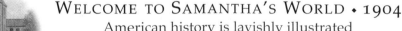

◆

WELCOME TO SAMANTHA'S WORLD • 1904
American history is lavishly illustrated
with photographs, illustrations, and
excerpts from real girls' letters and diaries.